MIRAGE OF BURNING THINGS

MIRAGE OF BURNING THINGS

RYAN DI FRANCESCO

Parlyaree Press
Atlanta, Georgia
www.parlyaree.com

Library of Congress Cataloging-in-Publication Data
Names: Di Francesco, Ryan, author.
Title: Mirage of Burning Things / Ryan Di Francesco
Description: First Edition | Atlanta : Parlyaree Press, 2026
Identifiers: LCCN: applied for | ISBN 9781961206342 (paperback)
Subjects: LCGFT: Poetry
LC record available at https://lccn.loc.gov/

Cover Image entitled "Operation Ivy" by Emily Andrews | www.emilyandrews.ca

Mirage of Burning Things is typeset in Claredon URW Ultra Narrow & Bogeda Sans.

No AI was used in the writing, editing, or production of this book.

Print ISBN: 978-1-961206-34-2
Ebook ISBN: 978-1-961206-35-9

For Bean.

MIRAGE OF BURNING THINGS
RYAN DI FRANCESCO

Table of Contents

Platform of the Last Train

shadows bloom
among

bent
blankets

in folded
fields

under
sunshine

slipping
across

lit mouths
blowing

the dimming day
beyond

the curve
of reality

roughed up
between bodies

and roots
of earth

writhing
like fossil veins

dancing on
shop windows

moving as
embers

across endless
concrete

past drifting
strangers

under the enlarged
pale sun

lifting dire dreams
from pockets

by spent
fingertips

beneath the skeleton
moonlight

poking
a burnt-out fire

dipping
underground

to catch the
last train

tonight
as it watches

from
the platform

like it's waiting
for you

in a fresh
suit

tailored
for now

whispering:

hello

delicately

The Eroded

The world balanced
on steel needles
pressing down on people
like they're ceramic bells,
imagining fields
swallowing the city's rot,
hiding in the long grass
with dead relatives
blowing out candles—
looking for membranes
grown across mouths,
torn from one another's teeth years before,
sifting through decay, fishing
for unclenched flowers,
gleaming under
drowned moonlight.

It's so lovely.

Like stitching Van Gogh's ear
back on in an alley
listening
beneath the sleepless, endless

sun

as if there is anything after laughter—
underneath
bloodless petals and broken glass
across narrow paths
of lifted

images

descending over heads
rooted in a different
time

collecting lost bones
in ploughed graveyards

as the lopsided night drew away
from the earth
felled
with us all.

The Leftovers

The beach is closed and the image of the polluted bay
reminds me of an old postcard / all still and perfect /
like a Lawren Harris or Tom Thomson painting
of the gentle north shore rising
where the women of the twenties once walked
in the young summer, twirling white parasols
finger by finger, talking about *St. Martin-in-the-Fields*
and the duty of helping the poor / leftovers /
strewn like broken ornaments
along a future of sick children in redbrick cities
boxed up on avenues reserved for the few

sparkling like glints of light in the fog

wishing for a happy ending in one of those timeless films—
like *Night of the Living Dead* or *Eraserhead*

always playing in this theatre

Mirage of Burning Things

so the house is still there

without me / and all the letters in the alphabet / and

there's got to be more to it than that / there's got to be more
to it than underground
rituals in waves of light / between zodiac creatures
waiting around the wooden tables afraid of touch / beside
shapeless
fires / fragments of a childhood / among branches / under
an orchard tree / in caves / among striped patterns of lilies /
in search of animal
skin attached to a popsicle stick / in search of

a chunk of heart wrapped /

in pink sun / rivers / pressed / latched onto
me / them / in the open mouth of the caged / bluebird / egg /
enclosed by dots and letters / by dots and

claws multiplied by faint smells / territories /
of fish / antlers / inside
the ribs of golden / grandeur / inside the ribs of cities
in dust / inside the rib of you / me and the cat licking its paws
after eating a cricket pulsing

in august nights / starved /
at the roadside zoo / reflected in teeth

Efficiency

I watch
the white swan

under
the new moon

and wonder
if only

we shared
the same vocabulary.

Then I would
ask if it loves

this beautiful
world

or knows about
decay

sleeping
on the lake

while joggers
run past me

yelling
about how

so-and-so at work
is efficient

how so-and-so is
a fucking shill.

But I couldn't care less
about shills

or efficiency

watching the swan
unfurl its wings

slowly
beating thunder

as it lifts
—then lifted—
into the sky.

Like it was meant
for this.

Too Young to Hear

Sitting on my
couch

listening to
church bells

toll in my
neighbourhood

while I finish
eating

two hard-boiled
eggs

half
an avocado

pineapple
strawberries

on a Sunday
morning

with its cool sleet
slapping the city

imagining
steam

rising from
espresso machines

in James Street
cafés

serving
the well-groomed

bending necks
raising cups

to lips
blowing

on the surface
laughing

and talking
where just around

the corner
a child

was stabbed
to death

at a school
parking lot

I pass
every day

walking
my dog

in a silence
I was once

too young
to appreciate

Tenderness: Part 1

She walked into the living room
and saw the white peonies
on the table
from the Farmers' Market

finally opened.

She said she wished
she were a snail
and could sleep
in all those petals,
wrap herself in them
in the middle of a dream.

Then she went to the kettle
to make peppermint tea.

And I thought:

I will write a poem about this
and stab the page

with a little tenderness.

For once.

Tenderness: Part 2

White peonies
at the bottom
of the garbage bag,

petals scattered
among coffee grounds
and rotting bananas,

were the prettiest
flowers
on our kitchen table
this summer.

Only days ago,
she asked
if they were real.

Like love.
Like poetry.

It ends.

All the Damn Way

the city
cracks open

another block

of abandoned
houses

with beaten faces

dragged
by suits

to the fence

of the encampment
reaching out

to hold time

in the broken
clouded

trail of strangers

passing by
groomed

for tomorrow

wishing all
a nice day

until it's not

until you're
drunk at noon

dropping

groceries
in a long line

with your clothes

covered in paint
complaining

about all this rain

about how it's got
to warm up

eventually

one would think
considering

how to end it all

while children
continue to

chuck rocks

into the garden
screaming

all the damn way

until recess
is over

and the one flower left

is picked
and will never have

been missed

Naked Fish

so many good
goddamn people

have it so hard here

climbing those
broken escalator steps

while waves foam
violently against

the buildings along
the closed street

with its warning signs
all around us

in this winter
existence

pretending
it's summer

year round

weeping like a wounded act

stuck

in between stacked bricks
and walls of snarls

as the sun dips
its face into
the great lakes

to catch a glimpse
of all those naked fish

like an image pulled from life
like a baby carriage
in front of a worn
tent at the park

where a woman
stood

and smiled
at me

once

and all I can remember

now

is the kindliness
in her eyes

shining brighter
than the flashy RE/MAX billboard

in the distance
lit above her

guaranteeing expert advice
alongside a 6-pack of quality pilsner

to soften the blow.

Decay

blistered hands
scraped against

cement

pulling
hollow beds

hung out
the window

of decay

as stomachs
pile up like worms

falling into
brief sunsets

sagging

more beautiful
than all

the people

remaining

Putting Her Face On

she fell
into an

empty vase

with murky
rose water

and

drowned
in sorrow

again

wandering in
the autumn

streets behind

her eyes
spilling onto

hardwood

standing
in a puddle

of nightmares

mourning
herself

before

putting her
face on

for work

as if it were
her choice

Fields

people in the field
down the street

from my apartment

squat through
the winter

until bulldozers

come in the spring
with a new navy wave

rushing

across their
bodies

scattering

leftovers from
the eaten dream

with those indomitable

black boots
dragging

desperation

hands
seized up

rising

then falling
like fists

in tents

bleeding
in the rain

scrubbing scars

from the city's
trepanation

but they return

sitting at the edges
in summer

finches

in their nests
waiting

under the mired sky

with nowhere
left to go

buildings always

punching down
with no one speaking

to each other

as the sun dirties
its face

along the rotten curb

punching up
with madness

made violent

by brushing
shoulders

with strangers

in line
departing

never to

reappear
so goddamn tired

Stems

what's left
has been
erased

picked

and scraped
from sludge
skinned

through
the gutter

rising
like stems

torn

from the roots
of the eye

turned inward
where

the vein
is clamped
to the starved

unseen

and still
surfacing

in my throat

Sanity

the late-night trains
and city lights
flicker

in and out
of chimneys

broken
like teeth

scattered
across pieces
of concrete

cornered
along the back alley

rippled
with spray-painted messages
behind the Portuguese cafés
at dawn

pouring flesh
into a clatter
of morning hell

grinding down wounds
sliced at the butcher
tossed
on a scale
at a dim downtown market

pretending

some dumb
sanity

parked on a hill
collecting grime

waiting

without eyes
or tongue

for the faceless hours

to finally wake up
from this
unnameable place

of flies
and blizzards

and move again
like invisible rain

and move again
like shadows

collapsing
under roofs

and move

again

You Don't Have to Go to the Movies to See the Horror

—THE FUTURE IS HERE
reads the sign
hanging from a dead pine tree

beside fenced-in, boarded windows

with no view—
born of a nineteenth-century vision,
now stinking of twenty-first century rot

where jobless buddhas
slump on a bench

talking about
the last night on earth

and how we're all ready
and not ready enough

for the foreclosure notices
and the brightness of horror

no one notices
on a kind day.

Like insects
circling a wine bottle.

Like a pair of shoes
drooping from a wire.

Like one side of a mouth
waiting at the hospital

in the long line
growing—

madly.

I'm So Glad

the dark
lake

slipped across
throats

dropped
in a cold

harbour
between pylons

near
the legless train

wrapped
in winter's fist

punching
that whispering

floor
where dire

wolves lie
moaning

until the day is
wrung out

laughing

the most
terrible
laughter

like there's one
gasp left

to remind us
why

we bother
at all

Golden Horseshoe

I go into the circling morning
happening again

       like footsteps
          in a hallway

and have a vision of you there
       at your desk on Saturday
          in front of your screen
              with your anxiety

while I walk slowly
          with our dog in the park
lifting her over a broken glass pipe
       then passing
          a pile of human shit

with high-rise buildings climbing in the distance
       looking so pretty and silver
          above bodies sprawled

          in the shape of a golden horseshoe
          all bundled up
       in yesterday's moon still
broken like peanut shells
       left in grandstands
when the fight is over
       and everyone leaves
          and goes home
       to sleep on comfortable mattresses

like we do
       even though
          with all that softness under warm sheets
my head still spins slowly at 3 a.m.
       all alone
          waiting
to go belly up in the night

waiting

for the end of the line   / with you /

For Lorca

Walking around,
thinking about that poet in New York
while roosters hide in tents
with masked and dented
dreams fleeing
tombstones
placed flat
instead of upright
in the street,
waiting
for fire escapes
in the downtown din
of the brain
with helicopters
searching for patterns
to appear

trying to make sense
of words
wrapped in a keen blade
of love,
circling the square,
arriving
again

on a path with less meaning
than a white plastic pail
tied to a tree branch,
swinging
in the slanted sun's
orange dust

out of reach
from empty grocery carts
in encampments
with heads jammed
in the moan of a radio,

starved and depraved,
waiting
like a sad and beautiful
cherry blossom tree
for warm weather in April,

along the very thin line
that separates
the million-dollar
bayfront homes
from
the less
who were,
a short time ago,
children

sobbing, stuck
in the grass the geese eat

valued less than
a box of rusty nails at a flea market,

wishing it were all over,
encased
in a threshold of
swollen defeat
inside government buildings
and city drop-in centres

like leaves blowing through
a trail of letters
leading home

or back to the liquor store

with enough change
to buy a cheap sherry
knowing
outside isn't going anywhere.

3-5 AM

Was up from three to five again.
Took a few zolpidem. They didn't help.

I'm tired of this insomnia.

I tell people. They say they can't sleep either.
I say I have insomnia. They ask if I've tried magnesium.

I smile.

You know, I have read poems in high-tier journals with whimsical lyric
turning insomnia into a pearl sky.
Those poems make me sick.

There is nothing beautiful about it.
It deserves plainspoken English. Or

an image: a bluff.

See the bluff? It's there.

I lie awake with a mouth full of rocks.
The sky is dark. The ocean is violent.
I watch the waves crash. They make no sound.
I can't spit the rocks from my mouth.
But I try.
I can't choke on them either.

I get a rush of thoughts to go all the way with it.
I get them.
But I don't have the guts.

I don't have the guts.

I didn't go all the way with it today.
My day ended with strawberry-rhubarb pie on the front porch.

I like strawberry-rhubarb pie.
I love her more.

It tasted better than the rejection from a Berlin journal
I woke to find in my email.
I sent them a packet of my best poems.
After that rejection, I sent my chapbook to small press in
Ontario.
It was rejected five minutes later: *appreciate the opportunity!*
but going to pass on this; sorry ...

I wanted to send a note saying: *thanks for reading.*
But I didn't.

I am tired. I have to teach soon.

It's my forty-fifth birthday.

Maybe this year will be better. Maybe not.
One day I won't be here. That thought comforts me.

It feels cool like those rocks on my tongue.
It sits in my belly like that pie.

I see the waves below.

Animal Dreams of Other Animals

as the cells flow backwards
and time circles under these lights
on the white floor / they enter /

one by one / shining

polyester insects / confined to plain skin / voices attached
pulsing like cicadas / still surfacing

in a typical morning / streaking across cement paths

collapsing inside the decaying buildings in me
with my neck
against the back of this chair

hiding in common corners / collapsing
into dim capsules / to wait and wonder

what shapes were put inside the first box / bent
like bodies inside a box /

multiplying everywhere

in this animal dream of other animals dreaming
for tunnels / burrows / covering
and uncovering myself
watching the life drain out from a needle

leaking

out like laughter / like soles over graves
on afternoon walks under yesterday's twilight

too quick for us / streaking across / skulls
under wired masks
until it's time to leave
to form lines / whipping through concrete

creatures / wrapped / scowling

as animals dream of other animals
dreaming of me dreaming

/ this /

silently

Notes:

Grateful acknowledgment is made to the following publications where some of these poems
first appeared, sometimes in earlier or slightly different forms:
• "The Eroded" and "Mirage of Burning Things" – Acta Victoriana
• "For Lorca" and "The Eroded" – Pacific Review
• "The Leftovers" – Ahoy
• "Platform of the Last Train," "The Leftovers," and "Mirage of Burning Things" – Azarão
• "You Don't Have to Go to the Movies to See the Horror," "Fields," and "All the Damn Way" –
Rawhead Journal
• "Too Young to Hear" – Bicoastal Review
• "All the Damn Way" – Bitter Melon Review
• "Efficiency" – The Amphibian Literary & Art Journal
• "Putting Her Face On" – Shine Quarterly
• "A Little Tenderness: Part 1" and "A Little Tenderness: Part 2" – The Orange Rose
• "Decay" – SQUID Magazine
• "Naked Fish" – SQUID Magazine
• "Golden Horseshoe" – Ivy Literary Journal
• "Sanity" – Milwaukee Avenue Messenger
• "3-5 AM" – MIDLVLMAG
• "I'm So Glad" – Blood + Honey

ABOUT THE POET

Ryan Di Francesco (he/him) is a Canadian writer, teacher, and editor based in Ontario. His work has appeared in over forty literary journals and anthologies, including Acta Victoriana, Pacific Review, Soliloquies Anthology, and Pinhole Poetry. He is the Editor-in-Chief of Shadow and Sax, an independent literary and arts press. His chapbooks include Skeleton Mine Disaster (Bottlecap Press) and The Paper Hound and Canadian Classic (Alien Buddha Press). He was shortlisted for the Rhonda Gail Williford Poetry Prize.

Founded in Atlanta, Georgia in 2023, PARLYAREE PRESS is dedicated to publishing writing that expands, reveals, and interrogates the mainstream. We seek out fiction, creative nonfiction, and poetry that exists in the liminal space between what was and what will be.

The cant of circus performers, freaks, queers, and thespians, Parlyaree is the invented language required to tell the stories of those othered, to keep their secrets, to keep them safe. It is a polyglot of experiences that may only be told in one's own voice. Parlyaree—as an invented language—borrows from what was to create something new.

That is what excites us at Parlyaree Press. Stories that transform; essays that reimagine; poetry that takes us behind the stanza to the core of our being and back again; language that plays as much as it conveys.

Writers: tell us your secrets.
Readers: reimagine your worlds.